ADOPTING PETS

ADOPTING PETS

HOW TO CHOOSE YOUR NEW BEST FRIEND

BY BILL GUTMAN

ILLUSTRATED BY
ANNE CANEVARI GREEN

Pet Friends
The Millbrook Press
Brookfield, Connecticut

The author would like to thank Linda Rice-Mandigo, Bob DeFranco, and Martha Wyss for not only sharing their experiences in animal rescue, but for giving their time and efforts in helping to keep their no-kill animal shelters running and working diligently to adopt out to good homes as many dogs and cats as they possibly can. Their work, along with that of countless others, is of the utmost importance in the battle to save the growing numbers of homeless animals.

Library of Congress Cataloging-in-Publication Data

Gutman, Bill.
Adopting pets : how to choose your new best friend / by Bill Gutman.
p. cm.
ISBN 0-7613-1863-1 (lib. bdg.)
1. Dogs—Juvenile literature. 2. Cats—Juvenile literature.
3. Dog adoption—Juvenile literature. 4. Cat adoption—Juvenile literature. 5. Animal shelters—
Juvenile literature. [1. Pets. 2. Dog adoption.
3. Cat adoption. 4. Animal shelters.] I. Title.
SF426.5 .G868 2001
636.7'0887—dc21
00-058241

Published by The Millbrook Press, Inc.
2 Old New Milford Road
Brookfield, Connecticut 06804
www.millbrookpress.com

CONTENTS

INTRODUCTION

If you like animals and have ever been to a pound or animal shelter, what you see there will break your heart. You will see dozens of unwanted dogs and cats looking out at you from cages and fenced-in runs with pleading, soulful eyes. Almost all of them want one thing. They want someone to take them home and give them a secure, safe, and loving life.

This scene is repeated in small towns and large cities across the country. Pounds and shelters are overflowing with dogs and cats that no longer have a home. Some are found alone and wandering the streets. A few have been injured in accidents—hit by cars—or in fights with other animals. Others are lost and have owners who can't find them or don't even try. Then there are unexpected litters of puppies and kittens, often born in the homes of people unable to care for them. Most of the animals, however, are brought in by their owners, who, for one reason or another, no longer want them. The problem is that there are far too many unwanted pets than waiting homes.

Because of this, thousands upon thousands of these young, healthy animals are euthanized every year. Euthanasia is a big word that means, simply, killing humanely. That's right, so many

7

dogs and cats are in need of a home that there is no place to keep them housed and fed while they wait to be adopted. Many of these unfortunate animals are then put to death. This problem has been with us for many years and is not getting any better. To put a young, healthy animal to death is a tragedy. It should not have to happen. Fortunately, many people throughout the land are trying to help.

This book will deal with the problems of unwanted dogs and cats, and show how you can help. If you or your parents want to get a pet for your home, you should think seriously about adopting one. Unwanted dogs come in all shapes and sizes, and a good animal shelter or rescue league will match the right dog to you. It's the same with cats. You can find a playful kitten or a quiet older cat. By giving an adopted pet a good home you may be saving its life. At the same time, you are opening a spot at the shelter for another unwanted pet so it too will have a second chance.

CHAPTER ONE
TOO MANY ANIMALS

Statistics never tell the whole story. However, in this case they are important. While the numbers can vary, they serve to point out the problem of too many pets and not enough homes for them. Just look at a few facts:

Every day more than 10,000 people are born in the United States. During that same 24-hour period, more than 50,000 puppies and kittens are born.

One female cat and her offspring can produce 427,000 cats in just seven years.

One female dog and her offspring can produce 67,000 dogs in six years.

An estimated 65 million cats are roaming the United States without homes.

The National Audubon Society estimates that cats kill 6 million birds a day in North America.

Though estimates vary, it's felt that as many as 10 million pets, maybe more, are euthanized in the United States each year. This does not take into account the numbers that are abandoned and die alone, are victims of disease, of starvation, or are hit by cars.

These are frightening statistics because they describe a problem that seems to have no solution. If 10,000 people are born in the country each day, and 50,000 dogs and cats are born during that same 24-hour period, how can there possibly be homes for all of them? If you have a dog or cat and give it a healthy, happy home, think how lucky that animal is. Your pet has a family to love it, good food to eat, a warm place to sleep, and will be treated by a veterinarian if it gets sick.

Unwanted animals do not have this kind of life. Some are struggling to survive on the streets or in the woods. Others are living in cages at shelters, hoping that someone will adopt them. When some shelters or pounds begin to overflow, some animals have to go. That's when they must be euthanized. It's a sad but true fact.

There are also, however, no-kill shelters. They do not euthanize dogs or cats. These shelters are committed to keeping each animal alive until a good home is found. However, no-kill shelters have limits. If there is no more room, they must refuse to take more animals in. Many of those animals are then taken to kill shelters. It's a circle that sometimes seems unbreakable.

THE NECESSITY OF SPAYING AND NEUTERING

Spaying and neutering are simple surgical procedures that prevent males from siring litters and females from becoming pregnant. For some reason, however, many pet owners are reluctant to have their animals spayed and neutered. Men sometimes think it's cruel to neuter a male dog. Others think females should have the joy of raising a litter of kittens or pups. Some people feel their children should see the miracle of birth through their pets, while others feel they can make money by continually breeding their female dogs and selling the pups.

People are reluctant to spay and neuter for still other reasons. Many of these are untruths that have been passed down for years. For example, some think a dog won't be a good watchdog if it is spayed or neutered. This is simply not true. A good watchdog will always be a good watchdog. Another claim is that a dog will become fat and lazy after being spayed or neutered. While

some animals do tend to put on some weight, increased exercise and less food will keep them in fine condition.

Still other reasons are offered for not spaying and neutering. None of the arguments hold up. The only reason not to spay or neuter a pet is if you and your family intend to become reputable breeders who will maintain the best standards of the breed with intelligent mating. Otherwise, there is no other reason for anyone owning a family pet or pets not to have each one spayed and neutered. Just that one act alone would greatly reduce the numbers of unwanted animals living in shelters or being euthanized each year.

CHAPTER TWO
WHY NOT ADOPT?

Anyone wanting to get a cat or dog for the first time should consider adoption. In fact, if you or your family want to add a second or third animal, adopting may also be the best way to go. Not only would you be helping to give an unwanted animal a home, but a good shelter can match you with a pet that's right for you and save you money at the same time. To consider adopting as an option, you would also be showing a responsible approach to having a pet. The lack of responsibility on the part of pet owners is another major reason for the existence of so many unwanted pets. It is important to consider these and other factors when deciding if adoption is right for you.

THE RESPONSIBILITY OF PET OWNERSHIP

It may come as a surprise to learn that not everyone who owns a dog or cat really loves the animal. Many people obtain an animal for the wrong reasons. Then, as soon as something changes in their lives, the animal is the first to go. Instead of thinking of their pet as a living thing—a family member with feelings, emotions, and needs—they consider it a piece of property that can be thrown away. It's almost like an old magazine. If you don't want it anymore, get rid of it.

"Owning a companion animal [dog or cat] is a lifetime commitment," says Bob DeFranco, president of the American Foundation for Animal Rescue in Rego Park, New York, and a trained animal behaviorist. "That animal has no one to depend upon but you."

Any person or family wanting a pet or pets must have the right reasons. Not only must they know which pet, or which breed, is right for them, but they must also know something about that animal and be willing to give it love, attention, and medical care for its entire life. To get a pet with the attitude that if it doesn't work out we'll just get rid of it means you are contributing to the huge problem of too many unwanted animals.

"I had a recent situation where a father brought a dog in to us that he wanted to put up for adoption," says Linda Rice-Mandigo, an adoption counselor at the Dutchess County S.P.C.A. in Hyde Park, New York. "He was a nice man who told me he got the dog for his three kids. But instead of making the dog an integral part of their lives, the kids were tying the dog up outside every afternoon when they came home from school and neglecting it. The father said it was his fault. Each of his children had his or her own color TV and computer in their rooms and had no time for the dog.

"I'm afraid we're developing a generation of kids who are 'possession people.' A dog becomes just another possession, like a Nintendo game. With a pet, the whole family should be involved."

The stories are endless. People continue to get animals for the wrong reasons, or simply get the wrong animal. Unhappy animals seldom spend their entire lives under one roof. Sooner or later they are loose on the streets or left on the doorstep of an animal shelter or dog pound. Others go from one bad owner to another. All these situations result from pet owners not accepting their responsibility, with the animals being put to sleep or put up for adoption.

THINK FIRST, ACT LATER

If you get a puppy or a kitten, that animal will have an average natural lifespan of between 10 and 15 years, sometimes longer. Will your home situation support this? If you have children who are 10 or older when you get the dog, chances are they will leave the house for school or to be on their own while the animal is still alive. Will someone in the household still be willing to care for the aging pet? If a pet is suddenly given up after many years it can be a devastating experience for that animal. If your children are older and want a pet, you might be better off adopting an older dog instead of getting a puppy that might be in the home longer than the children.

Many other important questions need to be answered as well. Do you live in a small apartment, or do you have a house with a backyard? If you want a dog, are you better off with a

small dog or a large one? Is someone willing to walk it when necessary? If it is a large, willful breed, are you willing to take the animal to obedience school? Do you know the characteristics of the breed? Is it hyperactive? Does it tend to be protective and aggressive? Does it need a great deal of hard exercise? Will someone be home most of the time so the dog doesn't have to spend long periods confined and alone?

If you don't think about things like this, you may be making a mistake. Get a dog for the wrong reasons, and it won't work. If you don't give a large dog enough exercise, it could become destructive in your home. If you tie a dog outside all day, it can become territorial and aggressive. If you leave your dog alone for long periods of time, it will be lonely and unhappy. In the wild, dogs are social, pack animals. When you get a dog, you become its pack or family. It wants to be near you and interact with you. It doesn't want to be tied to a doghouse, no matter how great that might be.

The same goes for a cat. The questions may be different, but they must be considered nevertheless. As a rule, cats are clean, quiet, and can be left alone more than dogs. They also use a litter box and don't have to be walked. But cats can also get into many things. They can jump up on furniture, put scratch marks on table legs, and knock things off desks, shelves, and just about anything else. If you have small animals in the house, such as birds or hamsters, the cat may decide to hunt. Once trained, however, cats can be a nearly perfect apartment pet.

If you live in the country you must watch your cat more carefully. If you let it out it can fight with other cats (especially if it's an un-neutered male), can begin to kill birds and other beneficial animals, and can be exposed to traffic hazards. So, once again, you must be sure to be a responsible and thinking owner.

Never make a hasty decision when getting a pet. Talk it over as a family. If you have questions, find someone who knows and

cares about animals. Never decide to "try it" for a while just to see if it works out. Be sure. If no one is home often, consider only animals that won't mind being left for periods of time. A cat is a better choice than a dog in this situation. These are all points that should be addressed before you get a dog or cat. Then, if you finally decide you will be a responsible owner and make a commitment to your new pet, you must make the final choice— to buy or adopt.

CONSIDER THE OPTIONS

People are getting dogs and cats all the time. Despite the overflow of unwanted animals, many thousands of people become pet owners each year. A large number of them are getting a pet for the first time. Others are getting a second pet, maybe a third. Some have decided to add a cat to a household that already has a dog. Others wonder about bringing a cat into a home that already has small animals, such as parakeets or hamsters.

The next question is: where to get the pet? At first, most people seem to want to start with a young puppy or a kitten. In some situations, however, an older animal will fit a person or family's needs better. Older dogs are usually housebroken and neutered. Older cats are quieter and not as wildly playful. Shelters often have puppies and kittens, as well. Adoption has certain advantages that everyone should know.

Unless you and your family have a good reason for wanting a certain kind of purebred dog or cat, you should seriously consider adopting. A no-kill shelter or animal-rescue organization will tell you about the dogs and cats they have for adoption and try to match the right one for you. These animals have all been checked by veterinarians and are usually up-to-date on their shots.

Most animals at a shelter have been through some difficult times. People who run the shelter want these animals to finally have loving, stable homes, so they try to make sure they are adopted by the right person or family. Because unwanted pets are so abundant, someone wishing to adopt will have a wide choice. With dogs, you can pick from large or small, puppy or older animal, a quiet or lively pet, a purebred or a mix. If you want to adopt, you aren't limited. You can go to a shelter and see which animal wins your heart. By adopting, you will not only provide a loving home to a dog that needs one very badly, but will also feel good in knowing that you have joined the fight to help the many unwanted animals.

The majority of cats at shelters are mixed breeds. Not as many people, however, look for purebred cats as for dogs. So it is important to consider adopting a cat because so many are available. Again, you will have a wide choice because the cats usually are of all ages and many pretty colors. There are kittens as well as older cats, and the people running the shelter will tell you if a cat is cuddly and affectionate, or more standoffish. They can tell you which ones are best suited for an apartment or for a rural setting, as well as which ones fit in best with other cats.

The bottom line is simple. If you and your family are sure you want to add a dog or cat to your household, think about adopting. If you do, you'll get a family pet that will give you years of unconditional love.

A FEW WORDS ABOUT BUYING

If you are deciding whether to adopt a dog, you might also be thinking about buying a puppy. Many people buy puppies when they could just as easily adopt. They may want a certain kind of purebred dog and will go to a breeder recommended by the American Kennel Club. This is fine if it's really what they want. They will probably pay a great deal for the dog, but will also know its "bloodlines." That means they will see the parents, and know if the animals have won ribbons at dog shows and are considered champions.

But the majority of people do it another way. They go to a pet shop. Today, pet shops are located in almost every large shopping mall in the country. Most of these have a puppy section, with a variety of purebreds in small cages behind a glass partition. Many families shopping at a mall on a weekend walk into these stores and look at the puppies. Maybe your family has even done it. If small children are with the family, chances are they will look at the cute, fluffy little pups and say, "I want one."

In this situation, people will sometimes buy a puppy on impulse. They will make a sudden decision about something they haven't thought about before. Out comes the credit card, and home goes the new puppy. Unfortunately, what seems like an enjoyable family outing resulting in a new pet often turns into a horrible, high-priced mistake. It can soon result in a bad situation for the animal.

Many problems come with buying a dog this way. For openers, you may not be getting a totally healthy animal. Most pet shops get their puppies from commercial breeders who turn out dogs the way a bottling plant turns out soda. The nickname for these breeding establishments is *puppy mills*. For years, reputable breeders and animal lovers have been trying to close down many of these "dog factories," or at least have more state and federal regulations placed upon them.

What exactly is a puppy mill? It is a place where dogs are bred strictly for profit and with very little regard to the breeding females, the safe handling of the puppies, or the socialization of the young animals. At a puppy mill, a female will spend her entire life in a small cage, being bred every time she comes into season or "heat." They will continue to breed the animal twice a year, never giving her a rest and with little or no regard to her health. It is a miserable life.

Puppy mills have been in existence since the 1960s when dogs were often bred for medical research. Now they supply puppies to the retail pet industry, notably pet shops. Many of these puppy mills breed dogs in dirty, unhealthy conditions. No

one knows how many dogs and puppies die there, never having a chance to find a home. Though they produce purebred dogs, the puppy mills take no pains to match up top-quality dogs so that they will produce the best examples of each breed — both in physical stature and personality. The parents are often mismatched.

Buying from a pet shop, you are also going to be paying as much as or even more than you would pay a reputable breeder. Chances are you will probably be talking to someone who knows very little about the personality of each breed. If something goes wrong with the purchase, it becomes your problem. Buying a dog from a pet shop is risky.

Such risks can be avoided by adoption. By deciding to adopt, you will come in contact with people who not only love dogs and cats but also give their time and effort to finding the right homes for animals that no one wants. Let's see how the entire adoption process works.

Chapter Three
ANIMAL SHELTERS AND RESCUE LEAGUES

Years ago, most stray dogs ended up in the pound. The images were of a dog warden catching stray dogs in a net and taking them away. Most were never seen again. Today, things are different. Towns still have dog wardens, but many of them work directly with private animal shelters and rescue leagues. Together, they try to save unwanted dogs and cats and help them to find new homes. While dog wardens are often paid by towns and cities, the shelters and rescue leagues rely on volunteers and private contributions to survive.

Those who work to save unwanted animals have a difficult job. Some work at shelters that are forced to euthanize animals. For them, seeing a healthy animal put to death is the most difficult part of their job. They continue their efforts, however, because they feel that some animals will be saved that otherwise might not. Those who volunteer at no-kill shelters try to rehabilitate and place their animals in good, loving homes. They do it over and over again.

Animal shelters are both large and small. The North Shore Animal League in Port Washington, New York, was founded in 1944 and has since found homes for some 800,000 animals. In 1998 alone, the League placed nearly 30,000 dogs and cats. It is a huge operation, which reaches out everywhere. At the other end of the spectrum are people who run small rescue programs from their homes, maybe keeping just a handful of dogs and cats. Every single rescue organization helps. In large cities the job is endless. The Friends of Animals Foundation in Los Angeles, California, is a perfect example. Founded in 1983 by Martha Wyss, the organization rescues and places homeless dogs and cats.

"We have room for about 125–135 animals," Wyss says, "and we're always at capacity. We probably get 30 to 40 calls a day asking us to take unwanted animals. It's simply impossible out here. The city estimates there are some 26,000 unwanted dogs and cats roaming the streets at all times. I would say that 70 percent of the calls we get, however, are from people who simply no longer want their animals. The other 30 percent are found on the streets."

According to Martha Wyss, the sad part is that most people make no attempt to solve the problems they might be having with their pets. Many find it easier to just give up their animals.

"They complain their dogs aren't housebroken or are chewing things," she explains. "Or maybe the dog nipped at a child. Some simply have the wrong breed for their situation. But the

fact remains that they get dogs, don't fully understand them, then don't have the time or desire to work with them and solve the problem.

"With cats, the common complaints are scratching the furniture, allergic owners, people moving and not willing to take their pet, and occasionally a cat nipping children. More cats seem to be abandoned than dogs."

The Friends of Animals Foundation has about 35 to 40 volunteers who help to socialize and rehabilitate the animals. They also have two kennel workers on staff and a professional trainer twice a month.

Bob DeFranco of the American Foundation for Animal Rescue says that New York City has similar problems:

"The biggest problem is that people don't realize the amount of attention dogs and cats need," he explains. "It's a big job that never ends, and when it becomes a burden, the animal is taken to a shelter or the pound. With dogs, the most common reasons people give up are behavioral problems that could be cured with training. However, taking the time to train the animal often interferes with the owner's lifestyle and out the animal goes.

"With cats, there is a problem of spraying urine if the animal isn't spayed or neutered. Cats are also very emotional, and things such as loud noises can throw them off. They don't like people being aggressive toward them and, under certain circumstances, can attack.

"Owning a companion animal is a lifetime commitment because that animal has no one to depend on but you. Many people don't realize that an animal has feelings and emotions."

The problem is the same in more rural areas. Only the source of unwanted animals is sometimes a bit different. The Dutchess County S.P.C.A. is located in Hyde Park, New York, some 75 miles (120 kilometers) north of New York City. The

mid-size city of Poughkeepsie is nearby, as are a number of small towns such as Pleasant Valley and Hyde Park. The no-kill shelter is almost always packed beyond capacity, with close to 200 animals, usually a few more cats than dogs.

Many of the animals coming into the shelter are strays and lost dogs, picked up by local dog wardens who work directly with the shelter. The S.P.C.A. doesn't take in many private surrenders. It has to be a special circumstance, or a dog that was adopted out from the shelter and, for one reason or another, is being returned.

"We see every kind of situation," says adoption counselor Linda Rice-Mandigo. "There are people who simply don't want to take the time to learn about and train their dog and people who flat-out lie. Then there are the tragedies, pets left behind when an owner dies and people who have lost their homes and are forced to move into motels. They want to take their animals and are heartbroken because they can't. Those we will take."

Rice-Mandigo sees a common thread running throughout. "The animals are never to blame. Strays that come in here aren't traumatized because this is often the best home they have ever had. They get regular meals, a warm place to sleep, and people who come in to show them love and attention.

"But the dogs who once had a good home and are now being let go, they are traumatized. They don't understand what happened to cause them to lose everything that was stable in their lives."

As with the others who see unwanted pets every day, Rice-Mandigo feels a lack of education and effort on the part of owners is the major reason for the growing problem. She says that people in the country often don't obey leash laws because they feel their dogs should be allowed to run. Animals that aren't spayed or neutered and on the loose will sooner or later sire a litter or become pregnant with one.

"When dogs in the country become lost, some people are heartbroken and make a big effort to find them," she says. "Others don't even bother, and some will actually curse you out because they have to pay a fee to get their dog from the pound or the shelter if we were lucky enough to find it. They blame the dog, so you know the kind of life the dog is going to have when it gets home."

Cats usually don't suffer the same kind of long-term abuse as dogs. "Cats will simply leave, while dogs won't," she says, referring to abusive situations.

Because they place value on their animals and also rely on donations to keep their organizations running, animal shelters will charge a modest adoption fee. The amount is not nearly that for buying a puppy from a pet shop or breeder. The fee charged by the shelter benefits everyone. In addition, there are a number of good reasons never to simply give a pet away.

WHEN "FREE TO GOOD HOME" IS BAD

Some people who decide they no longer want their pet will try to adopt it out on their own. How many times have you read the pet ads in your local paper and noticed one that begins: Free to Good Home? A bargain, right? A way to get a good dog and not have it cost anything? Unfortunately, nothing could be farther from the truth. Many people who decide to give their pet away have good intentions. What they can't control, however, are the people who call and say they want the animal.

The reasoning here is simple. If you don't put some kind of financial value on your pet, those who call to adopt might not put a value on it either. They may figure, *Hey, it's free. We'll try it for a while and if it doesn't work, we'll just get rid of it. Nothing lost.* A free pet can easily get passed on from one owner to the next. Worse

yet, a bad owner who doesn't understand the free dog, might simply abandon it.

There are still other reasons not to offer a pet for free. If you are giving away a purebred, someone might take it just to sell it for a profit. Still other unscrupulous people may try to sell the dog to a medical laboratory for research. This isn't legal, but it is one of the things you expose your animal to if you offer it for free. In some places, illegal dog fights are held for people to bet on. What better way to obtain throwaway dogs to be sacrificed for these fights than to answer a free pet ad.

A nominal fee of maybe $35 or $45 is not an outrageous price to put on any pet. Being willing to pay something for a dog will show good faith on the part of the new owner. Chances are much better that the dog will be taken care of, with good food and regular veterinary checkups. The pet will be inoculated against rabies and other diseases, and be checked for worms.

Another good idea is have the new owner sign an adoption agreement. That way, you will have his or her name and phone number. Tell them you will call to check on the dog, and include in the agreement that if the dog does not fit in the new home, it will be returned to you.

Remember, dishonest people are always looking to obtain animals for profit. People like this are much more likely to answer an ad that says: Free to Good Home.

Don't do it.

CHAPTER FOUR

GETTING DOGS AND CATS READY FOR ADOPTION

When a dog or cat arrives at an animal shelter, it is not always ready to be adopted. Without the efforts of shelter volunteers, animal behaviorists, and trainers, many of these animals would not be able to go back out to a family home. It is up to those giving their time to the shelter to determine an animal's needs and to rehabilitate it.

Most shelters have trained personnel who evaluate each animal. If the animal has behavioral or personality problems, they must be corrected before it is placed in a new home. Because of its limited capacity, Bob DeFranco of the American Foundation for Animal Rescue says his shelter won't take animals that are not adoptable.

"Some dogs, because of the way they have been treated, are too aggressive and will never be 100 percent adoptive," DeFranco says. "This is a small percentage, but it happens. For example, if a Rottweiler has been tied to a doghouse continually for three years with very little human contact, it is not likely going to be adoptable."

A major problem with dogs who have had a good home at one time and were suddenly surrendered is separation anxiety. The dogs are terrified of being abandoned again. When they are left alone, they often become destructive. They aren't getting even with their owners for leaving, as many people think. Rather, they are simply frightened. These dogs must have a home where someone will be with them a good part of the time.

It's tougher, as a rule, to place large dogs than small ones. The small ones usually go quickly, but large dogs can remain at a shelter for a year, sometimes two. Fortunately, people who run rescue shelters never give up. Bob DeFranco remembers a Labrador retriever mix that was at the shelter for nearly 18 months. It was finally placed with two women whose dog had died and turned out to be a perfect match.

Linda Rice-Mandigo says there is usually a good reason for an animal behaving badly. "We have had some dogs come into our shelter as fear biters and leave as wonderful family pets. . . . It just takes some real work by our staff and volunteers to allow the animal to regain its confidence and overcome its fears, which are almost always caused by mistreatment by its former owners.

"We have volunteers who have gone through a training course in animal evaluation," Rice-Mandigo says. "When the animals come in the evaluators will try touching them in different

ways, even pinching them and poking them a bit, just to see what might set them off and how they react to certain types of handling. That way, we'll know what to tell prospective people who come to adopt as well as working to modify the behavior."

CATS NEED REHAB TOO

Though cats do not have the same problems as dogs, they still get all the attention they need. Many cats have not been properly socialized. If they have run away, been abandoned, or become lost, they may be partially feral, or wild, used to surviving on their own without people.

"People come in to socialize the cats," Rice-Mandigo explains. "They touch them, brush them, talk to them, get them used to being around people once again. Since many cat owners have more than one animal, we also have to see how a cat will get along with other cats. It's pretty easy to see the kind of personalities they have. Some are mushy and want to cuddle with their owners. Others are standoffish. We have to know before we let any cat go out.

"Those whose personalities cannot be modified become barn cats, living on farms where they are needed to help control the rodent population. That way, they have a home, still live on their own, and perform a needed service. So we try anything. We never put an animal down. We're determined to find a way to allow every animal we take in to ultimately have a secure, safe life."

CHAPTER FIVE

PETS AND PEOPLE: MAKING A MATCH

The people who help adopt out dogs and cats probably take more pains to match their animals to prospective owners than anyone. They know the dogs and cats at their shelter need another chance. Sometimes it's more than a second chance. It may be a third, or even a fourth chance, and they want it to work. A person can't simply walk through the doors of a shelter, look at the animals, and say, "I want that one."

Every shelter has its own way of matching people to animals, but there are usually many similarities. Martha Wyss of the Friends of Animals Foundation in Los Angeles begins the process by spreading the word about the shelter and the animals they have for adoption.

"We advertise in the *Los Angeles Times* four days a week," Wyss explains. "We also have a Web site, put up signs, do telephone work, and appear occasionally on television."

People who come to the shelter to adopt are interviewed about their home situation and the kind of care they plan to give the animal. If they already have an animal, the shelter will ask them to bring in that animal so it too can be evaluated. They also want to see how the animal will react to the animal that is to be adopted out. In effect, they are trying to make sure the adoption will work.

"We always deliver the animal that is being adopted," Wyss says. "We insist on seeing the situation one of our animals will be going into."

That doesn't mean that everyone who wants an animal gets one. "We weed out many people right on the telephone," Wyss continues. "If they know absolutely nothing about animals, we don't really want them. If they say they are going to keep the animal outside all the time, we won't adopt to them. We stand behind all the animals we adopt out and we will take them back, even after five years."

It's a similar situation at the American Foundation for Animal Rescue. People wanting to adopt must fill out an application with references that will be checked. The Foundation wants all its adopted animals to live inside a house with its family. Animal behaviorists, such as Bob DeFranco, evaluate the situation to make sure that people are matched to the right animal.

"I would say that 75 percent of our adoptions work," DeFranco says. "If one doesn't we will almost always take the animal back, but we also work with people and expect them to make an effort to make it work."

Both Martha Wyss and Bob DeFranco have seen a similar phenomenon. If an animal is brought in that has serious injuries, or has been badly abused, or perhaps rescued from a precarious situation, it is adopted almost immediately, with many people calling about it.

"Any animal that gets media attention is adopted quickly," DeFranco says. "It's as if it gives people fulfillment to help, say, a dog that has lost a leg or a cat that has been burned. What they should realize is that all the animals need help."

KNOW WHAT YOU WANT

Those who want to adopt can help the matching process by knowing what they want before they go to a shelter. If a family is living in a small place and decides upon a small dog, they shouldn't change their mind because a big, lovable dog seems to like the kids. That same lovable dog may need a lot of room to run and exercise, something none of them can easily provide.

If your best friend has a dog and a cat at home and you only have a dog, you must be careful about adding a cat. It doesn't always work. That's why many shelters will want you to bring your existing animal to them before they agree to an adoption. If your dog has a history of chasing cats, chances are the two animals will not get along.

Families must also discuss possible negatives. If the kids forget to walk the dog, are the parents willing to do it? If a dog or cat puts some scratches on the parents' good furniture, are the kids willing to try to train it, or will the parents immediately return it to the shelter? If the dog vomits in the house, will the kids learn how to clean it up? An animal isn't like a toy. When you finish playing with it, you can't just put it away.

All these things should be decided before you even go to the shelter. Then an adoption counselor or animal behaviorist will work with you on a final decision. You will be asked again if you really want to adopt and will help get you the best animal for your situation. You have to trust their judgment. They do it every day, and they are only looking out for the welfare of the animal. You must remember that you are making a commitment to a dog or cat who has probably been let down once or twice before by its previous owners. You shouldn't let that happen again.

UNDERSTANDING YOUR ADOPTED PET

Whether you are adopting a dog or cat, or getting a brand-new puppy or kitten from another source, you should learn all you can about that animal. Both dogs and cats have a number of behaviors that they will bring to your home from the wild. They will do some of the same things their ancestors did thousands of years ago. The more you know about these behaviors, the better you will understand your pet. It's important for any animal you have, but especially important if you are adopting for the first time. The more you understand, the better chance there is for the adoption to work.

For example, you may take your dog outside one day, and, before you can stop him, he starts rolling in some very smelly stuff on the grass. He isn't doing this because he likes to be dirty. Sometimes, he may just find the scent very appealing, even though you think it's awful. But he may also be doing it for another reason. Dogs and wolves, in the wild, sometimes roll in

something with a strong odor to cover their own scent. That way, if they are hunting, their prey won't pick up their scent and run away. Though your dog isn't going hunting, the instinct to roll in different scents still remains.

Cats too have leftover behaviors from the wild. You might be sitting in your room one night doing your homework, when your cat comes in. To your surprise, she suddenly drops a dead mouse or other small animal at your feet. At first, you may think this is disgusting. To the cat, however, it is something else. Ancestors of the cat in the wild (including lions and tigers) are known to bring their prey to other cats as a social gesture. So your cat is simply bringing you a present. She likes you. Don't

scold her. Just dispose of the dead animal and understand why your cat brought it to you.

You can learn more about these animal behaviors by reading two previous books in this series, *Becoming Your Dog's Best Friend* and *Becoming Your Cat's Best Friend*. The more you know about your pet, the better owner and friend you will be.

CHAPTER SIX
WHAT YOU CAN DO

The problem of too many animals is not going to go away quickly. As with many other things, education is extremely important. Many people still don't realize how many unwanted animals are out there and how many are put to death. Even more frightening is the fact that many people don't seem to care. They feel it isn't their problem or, as mentioned before, animals are just another possession that can be obtained and discarded with no consequences.

If you are not familiar with the work done at animal shelters, then you should visit one. You can find a no-kill shelter in every city and town around the country. All of them encourage young people to come in and learn about the problem of unwanted animals.

"We had a Brownie troop come in recently," says Linda Rice-Mandigo of the Dutchess County, New York, S.P.C.A. "The girls saw all the animals at the shelter and we gave them information about how we work and about adopting. Many of the girls wrote us thank-you notes and told us about what they learned. I remember one writing that she didn't know cats couldn't live on their own in the wild."

Many shelters work directly with the schools in their areas. The feeling is that the more young people learn about the problem of unwanted animals, the better the situation will be in future years. Education is the key. People must begin to look upon animals as more than just possessions.

"We work directly with about seven or eight schools in Los Angeles," says Martha Wyss. "Many kids at the high school level are now volunteering their time and coming in to help. Younger children come in groups from the schools and we let them begin by working with the cats. The more they learn when they're young, the more they'll help when they get older."

If you start now, you can make a difference. Take good care of your own pets. If you are in a family situation where you can adopt, speak to your parents about it. Ask them to visit a shelter with you. If they don't seem to care about animals, tell them about the problem of unwanted pets.

Some shelters look for foster homes to take dogs and cats. The animal lives with you until a permanent home can be found. This isn't always easy because you may come to love the animal yourself. Sometimes you can adopt it. But when the shelter finds someone to take it, you must give the animal up. However, by loving the animal and working with it in your home, you will have helped make sure the adoption works.

There are other ways to help, as well. If you are volunteering at a shelter, try to get your friends to join you. If you have friends or relatives who won't have their pets spayed or neutered, talk to them about it. Many shelters have literature stressing the importance of spaying and neutering. You can help pass this literature to pet owners who don't realize the importance of this simple and healthful procedure. If you have to write a composition in class, write about the problem of unwanted animals.

Animals have been a part of the world before humans came along. Now, as more and more people inhabit the world, many species of animals are disappearing from the wild. Some have already become extinct. That means they have disappeared forever. Naturalists view this as a tragedy. Zoos are now breeding

wild animals in danger of disappearing, trying to preserve the species.

At the same time, our domesticated animals are still multiplying in numbers that are difficult to fathom. These are the animals that live with us and give us unconditional love and affection. It's almost bizarre that so many people worry about lions, tigers, gorillas, and other wild animals becoming extinct, but not about the problem of too many dogs and cats.

Yes, it is important to keep wild animals from disappearing. But it is just as important to save our domestic friends. Dogs and cats cannot be allowed to breed freely. People should work harder to solve the problems they are having with their pets. To do that, they should learn to understand and train them.

People should also support their local animal shelters and rescue organizations by helping to raise money and giving their time. The goal is to find good homes for these animals and good people to adopt them. That's the best chance these animals have.

FIND OUT MORE

WEB SITES

North Shore Animal League (New York) www.nsal.org
P.A.W.S.—Pet Adoption Web Site (Arizona) www.azpaws.com
Pets In Need (California) www.ÏPetsInNeed.org
San Francisco SPCA www.sfspca.org
Pet Rescue League (Florida) www.petrescue.com
Best Friend Pet Adoption (North Carolina) www.bfpa.org
Animal Adoption (New Jersey) www.animaladoption.com

BOOKS

The Adoption Option: Choosing and Raising the Shelter Dog for You. Eliza Rubenstein. Howell Books, 1996

Becoming Your Cat's Best Friend. Bill Gutman. The Millbrook Press, 1996

Becoming Your Dog's Best Friend. Bill Gutman. The Millbrook Press, 1996

Shelter Dogs: Amazing Stories of Adopted Strays. Peg Kehret. Albert Whitman, 1999

Saved! A Guide to Success With Your Shelter Dog. M. L. Papurt, Myrna L. Papurt. Barron's Educational Series, Inc., 1997

INDEX